C is for Charlemagne

A Historic Alphabet

by History Unboxed

THE ABCS OF CHARLEMAGNE Copyright © 2022 by History Unboxed
ISBN: 978-1-956571-11-0
Photo of Bertrada © Marie-Lan Nguyen / Wikimedia Commons
Photo of Aachen Cathedral Photo 9267732 / Aachen © Eyewave | Dreamstime.com
Photo of Interior Chateau de Chenonceau Photo 46504237 © Daniel M. Cisilino | Dreamstime.com
Medieval Scribe Illustration 38632068 / Book © Awcnz62 | Dreamstime.com
Crown and Book © Awcnz62 | Dreamstime.com

Cover Illustration by Matthew Maley

Inside this book you will find ornate illuminated letters and old fashioned looking script. Charlemagne's influence on the academic culture included a new style of handwriting, although Charlemagne himself was unable to write fluently. His head scholar, Alcuin, who ran the school at Aachen, was instrumental in the development of this script, called Carolingian Miniscule. Why did they need a new kind of writing? In those days, there was not a unified script in Europe. Local languages each had their own style of writing. This new venture attempted to create lettering that would reflect the Latin written language and be recognizable across Europe, no matter what the spoken language was in a given area. The letters persisted and had enormous influence on our modern lower-case alphabet.

This humorous alphabet book is perfect for sparking interest about the life of an influential, reformative, and sometimes violent king. Educator preview recommended for this text.

HISTORY
UNBOXED ®

A is for Aachen,
the cathedral he built

Charlemagne established a school at Aachen. Sons of his nobles went to the school. He also started schools for boys of all social classes.

B is for Bertrada,
his mother so dear

Bertrada helped keep the peace between Charlemagne and his brother, Carloman. They often argued when they were co-rulers.

C is for Carolingian
miniscule, the new
handwriting style

The new script saved room on the page. It was used in many texts. It preserved so much knowledge that people call it the Carolingian Renaissance. You are reading a Carolonigian Miniscule alphabet right now!

D is for Desiderata,
the first wife
he despised

Charlemagne married Desiderata to become an ally with her father. They did not get along. She left him after only one year.

E is for Einhard,
biographer and friend

His biographer, Einhard, was a close personal friend, and was quite honest about his goals in writing Two Lives of Charlemagne. He aimed to describe: "the extraordinary life of this most remarkable king, the greatest man of all those living in his own period,....together with his outstanding achievements, which can scarcely be matched by modern men."

F is for feudalism,
the system he
perfected

Feudalism is a social system. The king gave land to nobles called vassals. The nobles help the king fight his wars. Vassals let Peasants live and work on their land. The nobles are supposed to protect them in return.

G is for Greek,
one of the languages
he spoke

Charlemagne studied at his own palace school. He learned Greek and Latin. He spoke a dialect of German.

H is for Hildegard,
his favored wife and
mother of nine

Hildegarde,
Femme de Charlemagne.

Hildegard had nine children, including one set of twins. She often traveled with Charlemagne during their twelve years of marriage.

I is for insomnia,
his chronic struggle

Charlemagne often had a hard time sleeping. He kept writing materials under his pillow. When he couldn't sleep, he studied and wrote.

J is for Joyeuse
the sword

According to legend, Charlemagne carried a sword called Joyeuse, or joyful. "By his side hung Joyeuse, and never was there a sword to match it; its colour changed thirty times a day." (Song of Roland)

K is for knights and
the code he established

He was a warrior king. He inspired opinions on how kings and knights should behave. He was both fierce and merciful.

L is for Louis the Pious, the son who reigned next

His son, Louis the Pious became the
next king. Louis' sons divided the
kingdom after Louis' death.

M is for the Moors
whom he battled

Charles fought against the Moors. They had conquered Spain and North Africa. They were building a great Islamic kingdom. Not all the Moors were his enemies. He fought with one group of Spanish Moors against another Muslim kingdom.

N is for nobles,
who sent their sons to
his school

Their sons learned astronomy, rhetoric, and logic. Nobles came from all over Europe to study at his school.

O is for organization,
how he ran his large
kingdom

He ordered laws to be written down for the first time. He set up local governments.

P is for Pope Leo,
who crowned him
Emperor

Pope Leo III crowned Charlemagne as the Holy Roman Emperor. This is the Vatican, home of the Pope.

Q is for queen
consorts, of which
there were four

Charlemagne married four times and had children with five other women. He had eighteen children in total.

R is for Roland,
who inspired songs of
praise

Roland helped lead Charlemagne's army. He became a hero in medieval literature because of his bravery. "The Song of Roland" was composed about him in the 11th century. In the song, he fought bravely and died in battle.

S is for the Saxons
he slew

Charlemagne fought the Saxons for 30 years. He finally won and forced them to become Christian. Any Saxon who did not convert was put to death.

T is for tall,
for his great height

Charlemagne was tall. He was six feet tall. That was at least five inches taller than the average man of his time.

U is for unequaled
in influence

Charlemagne influenced education reform, legal systems, and religious practice. Modern people may not agree with his methods. But he changed Europe in many ways.

V is for Verden,
where the massacre
occurred

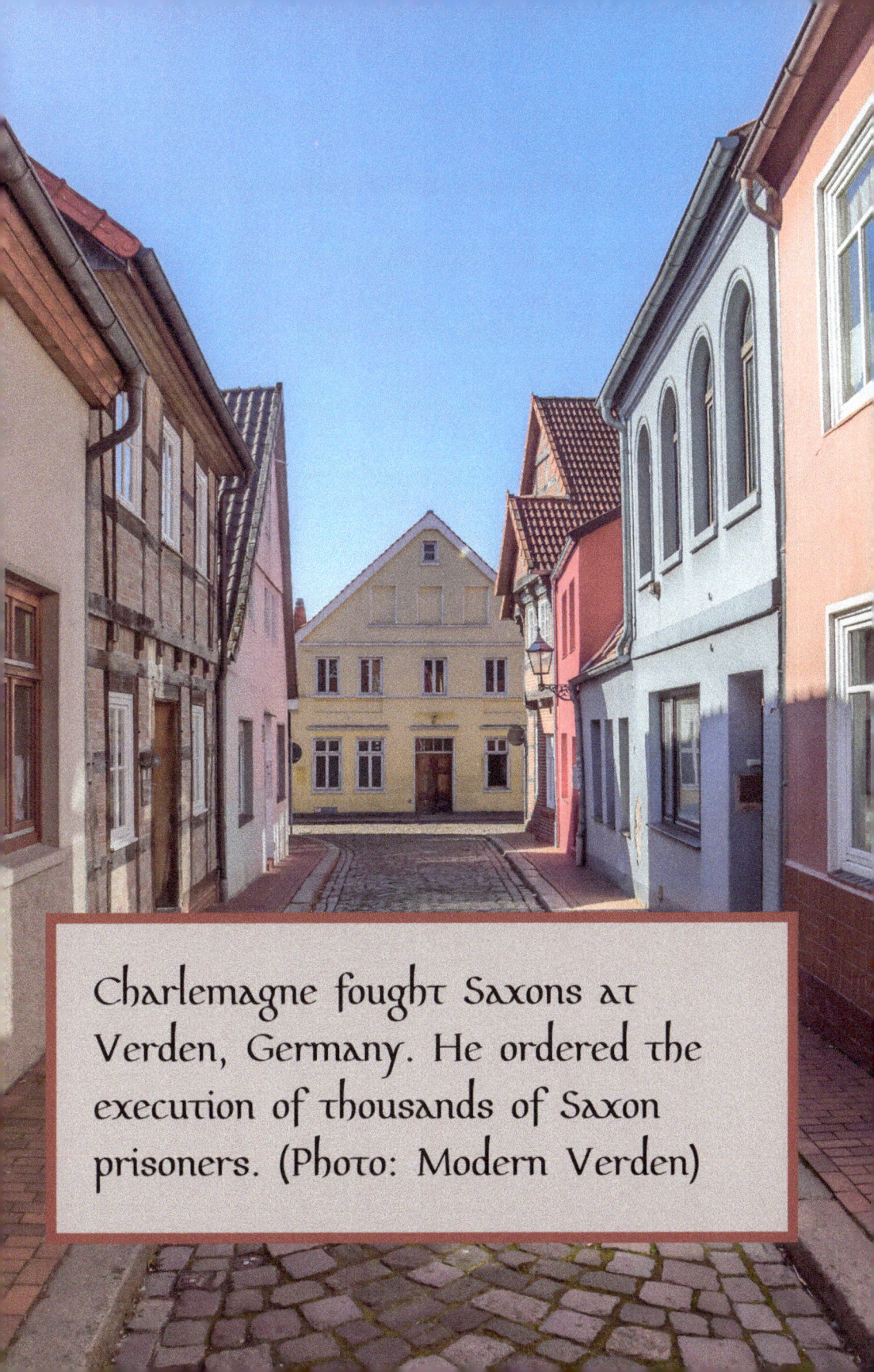

Charlemagne fought Saxons at Verden, Germany. He ordered the execution of thousands of Saxon prisoners. (Photo: Modern Verden)

W is for
Widukind, his
Saxon nemesis

Widukind was the Saxon leader. His name means "child of the forest." He became more of a mythical hero than a historical figure.

X is for the xylophone,
which he didn't invent,
and Xerxes, whom he
never met

Xerxes probably never held a xylophone either.

Y is for Young
Charles, who should
have ruled the Franks

Charlemagne had four sons by marriage. They were Pepin the Hunchback, Charles the Younger, Pepin of Italy, and Louis the Pious. Charles died of a stroke before his father's death.

Z is for Zachariah,
envoy to Jerusalem's
caliph

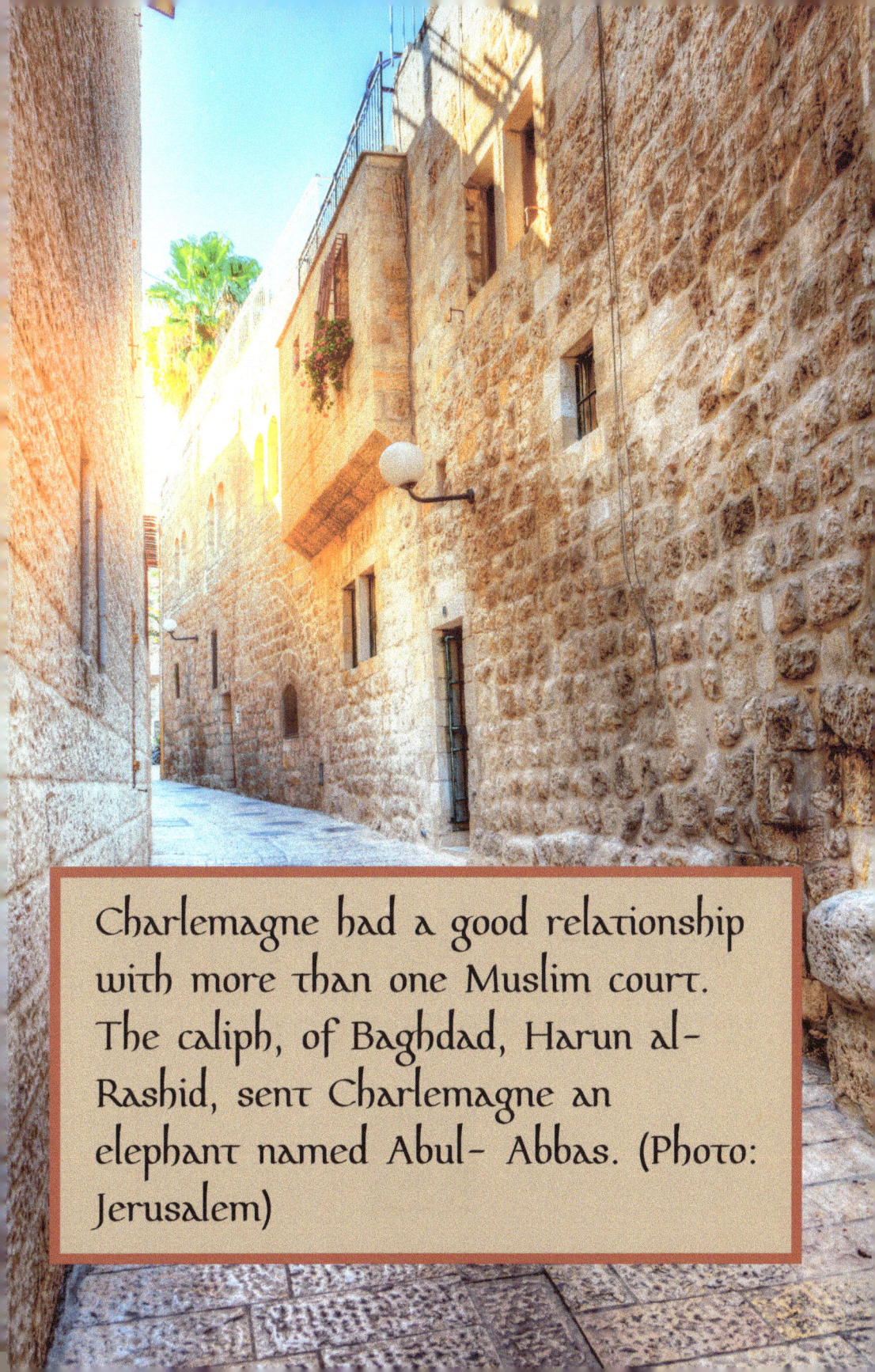

Charlemagne had a good relationship with more than one Muslim court. The caliph, of Baghdad, Harun al-Rashid, sent Charlemagne an elephant named Abul- Abbas. (Photo: Jerusalem)

To learn more about
Charlemagne and dive into
hands-on learning, visit
www.historyunboxed.com